Mason Jars

Mason jars come in a wide range of forms, styles, as well as sizes. If you have mason containers stockpiled, well and good, you can make use of the same. If you do not have mason jars, after that you need to make a purchase.

Where to Buy

You can start by going to a shop that concentrates on canning goods. Some can additionally be bought from thrift shops or pre-owned shops, even antique shops have mason jars. You can even locate it in your regional Wal-Mart. Yours genuinely was fortunate sufficient to rack up antique mason containers create flea markets and a couple of garage sales. Do not worry if the cover is missing or is in poor problem, you can always buy new ones. It's the bottle containers that are essential! Likewise, there is an expanding market for mason jars online, especially provided the huge rise of survival preppers and also artisan motivated house tasks. It is best to screw and order the rounded band rim from the very same location or on the internet store. This way, you make certain it will fit.

Sanitize the Jars

It is really crucial to disinfect your mason jars. Never ever re-use the round lids and screw bands. Constantly get new ones. This is regardless of its look. If a bottle has discoloration ingrained into the glass or has nicks, cracks, as well as chips, do not utilize it - period!

Just how do you sterilize mason containers?
1. Wash with soap and water. Make certain to scrub off any type of dust,

corrosion, crud, food particles, etc, that is stuck to the mason jar.

2. Soak in chlorine mixed water. 1 tablespoon per litre of water used.

3.Re-wash like previously.

4. This action is to be done quickly prior to positioning the ingredients right into the mason container. In a large pot, put the bottles as well as totally immerse in water. Don't include the lid and band. Partly immerse the tong you will certainly utilize later.

5. Allow the water boil as well as wait 10 minutes prior to switching off the heater. Not to fret, mason containers are constructed from tempered glass and can withstand this amount of heat. Although, it is best to make use of a dual walled pot. Allow the water cool.

6. Reserve a clean towel. Clean your hands. Currently secure the tongs. Utilize it to remove the jars. Area bottom up on the damp towel and let dry for a minimum of 5 minutes.

7. Clean completely dry with a tidy fabric. If you have a dishwasher with dryer feature, after that you can utilize the very same to entirely dry each glass. At this point you position whatever you intend to place within, as well as secure it with a brand-new rim and cap. You can then include the decorations after it has actually been sealed. For designs that will certainly take you a long period of time to finish, far better seal the jars now and then only open it after the style has actually been finished.

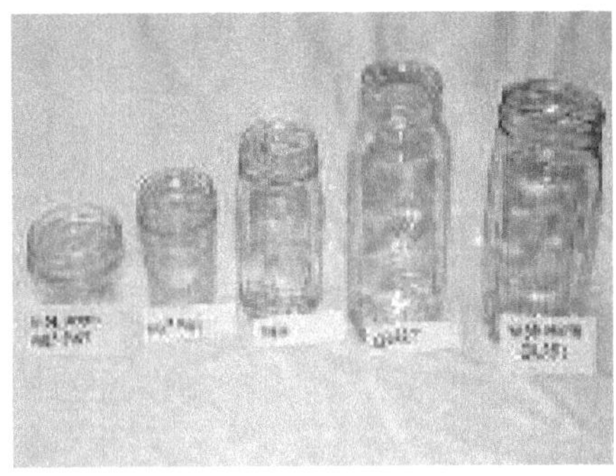

Design Ideas

The possibilities are limitless. You can repaint your mason jar. You can include dimension to it by utilizing adhesive stick. You can utilize gooey t-shirt printing paint to stylise your mason containers. You can likewise tint the exact same. Some even cover their mason jar with its own knitted sweater!

Suggestion: Take numerous jars and also use them as testers. Enjoy with the designs and also make use of a number of methods or craft materials to see what works as well as what looks great.

The only important thing to remember is to utilize food quality products accepted by the FDA. Just touch or make layouts outside part of the covers as well as cups, as well as just when the same is appropriately sealed. Do not touch the screw leading area!

Don't quit with developing the jar. Embellish the rim and lid as well. Again, be sure that the cover is firmly shut. Do not repaint the within portion of the same. With that said in mind, you can utilize your glue gun to cover the lid with ribbons. You can even use very adhesive to add a porcelain figurine or toy figure on top, and then leave as is or paint the whole point with a single layer of paint.

Cover any Openings

If you are going to repaint the cover, it would be best to cover the little hole created inside the container as well as the edge. Utilize your adhesive gun for this. Afterwards, you can constantly peel it off. Simply make certain not to place the dissolved glue stick deep inside the hole, so it's less complicated to get rid of. Later on, you can also points out with a paint brush.

Tip: spray paint is best done outdoors, as well as far from any type of flammables. Shake the paint can as well as comply with the directions published on it i.e. the spray nozzle ought to be around one foot far from the container.

Repaint Brush

For an extra artisan feeling, make use of a paint brush. You can make use of the broader brushes to cover huge locations and after that the better ones for the information.

Including Shapes, designs and also letters

Use your adhesive weapon with stick to create letters. Develop numbers, or include styles. No need to be spotless or be completely also. The lopsidedness contributes to the appeal. Paint over the letters, and viola, you've obtained a very stylized mason container. You can also purchase ornamental items create cross sewing shops as well as paper tole shops.

Mason Jar Designs

Some jars are just made, while others have designs, printed tags, and also a take care of. There are also a number of sizes to select from. It's up to your use, creative thinking and also preference.

You also have the choice of leaving the container undecorated. In which situation, it would certainly be best to put added initiative on the cover and also edge. This is normally done if the food items within are colorful.

Tips, Tricks and Techniques

Let's be sincere right here, you are on a time problem. You have your work suitable you baking and also embellishing your mason jar. Likewise, if you need to pick up a digital book in order to get baking recipes, after that opportunities are you aren't the established baker. That is why, it is highly a good idea that you take ideal shortcuts that do not compromise the quality of your job, and enable you to actually bake tasty goodies.

Work Smart

Usage readymade items i.e. dough, crust, mix and also bake muffin or cake dough, and so on. Take for instance, apple pie; have you any concept how hard it is to make a collapse to the touch pie dough? It's messy, time consuming, as well as costly. On the other hand, you can buy readymade pie dough for a portion of the time as well as cost.

Beta Test

Always try a little batch prior to cooking your huge batch. Always have 1 mason container, per set for tasting. Keep in mind, if this is your very first time, comply with the guidelines word for word.

Health Is Key

If you want your food to last, you ensure you utilize tidy cooking equipment as well as utensils. Never double dip a spoon. Constantly wash your hands. And also never ever area craft product near cooking/baking materials.

Tidy, Bake after that Decorate

As a basic regulation, you want to clean up the mason jar, cook whatever gift you

desire o bake, seal and embellish. This implies you decorate quickly. This is possible, offered you already recognize what you are doing i.e. beta tested your designs.

Use a Thermometer

Interior pie temperature in the middle is around 170 to 180 degrees F. Let cool type the oven for 5 to 15 mins. This will certainly reduce the risk of the mason jar cracking from. Leave the door available to let as much heat bent on lessen over baking.

Temperature Spikes
Mason containers can hold up against boiling water for several mins. What it can not endure are sudden changes in temperature level i.e. right from the oven and onto freezing room temperature or worst, the refrigerator. If it is coming out of the stove, ideal leave it there up until it slowly cools. Partially opening the oven door allows you to quicken the change process.

Detailed Instructions

upply a warning to the moms and dads and the child. The steel parts as well as decorations should be eliminated before reheating or microwaving. Now write down or print out straightforward guidelines. Ideal affix this on the cap by pinning the directions in between the steel edge as well as the lid. If you are tinning the things, then use dual sided tape of straightforward paste to glue the directions on the cover.

THIS SUMMER,
LIVE LIFE. FULL
SPEED. ONE S'MORE OR
TWO, AT A
TIME.

Recipes for the Kids

Let's begin with things you can do when you are in a hurry! The situation is, you have your mason containers but you have less than 12 hours to go. What do you do?
You will certainly need great deal of different sweets, candies, or miniature cookies, an adhesive gun with stick or Crayola craft paste, craft paper or cloth ribbons, and also a couple of Christmas inspired decors. You do not have much time so you concentrate on getting colorful foodstuff to place within.

1. Locate a way to fill up the mason jars with sweets as well as sweets in a manner that looks imaginative i.e. layering is always an excellent suggestion.
2. Shut the cover snugly, yet not too tight. Bear in mind, kids are mosting likely to open it!
3. Use your adhesive stick or craft paste to compose the name of the recipient on the mug. You can add basic decorations like celebrities, dots, doodles, etc. Paint over the glue stick. It ought to currently be vivid on its very own if you are taking legal action against craft paste.
4. Allow dry for 10 to 20 mins.
5. Utilize your artisan paper or outfit to cover the lid and also edge of the cup. Your goal is to keep the level portion as cool as feasible and to make expert looking folds up. Pointer: square shaped paper or dress works best.
6. Tie something around the rim to hold points in position and for added impact. Connect a devotion card that also includes directions on exactly how

to maintain the components fresh i.e. refrigerate after opening up.

Mix, Stir, and also Microwave
Exactly how around you provide the contents and allow the recipient make the real materials. This is specifically interesting youngsters that have an analytical side in them. The vital thing is to make it basic, edible, and yummy. This is a treat so you don't intend to be extremely health mindful, but you also don't intend to wreck their health and wellness, or make them into sugar thrill beast that leave a path of destruction.

- cupcakes in a box (mix and also bake) Chocolate chips as well as sprinkles

- Small zip lock containers for specific product packaging

Experiment on the sections by trying it out yourself on a tester mason jar. Area the parts inside zip lock bags. Give straightforward directions on how much water to make use of, the length of time to blend and how long to microwave or bake.

Include guidelines on just how to add the delicious chocolate chips, which can be mixed right into the batter and the sprinkles on the top.

Tip: Kids do not want something fancy. All they want is something pleasant, has lots of chocolate, and also is enjoyable to make. Add color to the mix by repacking vibrant sweet confectionary, chocolate chips, or perhaps an Oreo cookie collapse to place on top.

Mason Jar S'mores

Graham crackers Sugar
Butter
Marshmallows (large white ones) Readymade fudge mix (any brand) Milk (optional).
Eggs (optional).

Absolutely nothing claims Holiday benefits than some smores! It's enjoyable and so very easy to make,.

S'more Crust:.
You will certainly require smashed Graham biscuits, sugar, and butter. The proportion is 3 is to 1 Graham biscuit is to sugar. If you can't discover the smashed variety, after that position several biscuits inside a zip lock back as well as crush. You will also require half a stick of butter (around 2 ounce) per 1 1/2 cup of Graham crackers. As an example, 1 1/2 cup of Graham biscuits need half a cup of sugar and also half a stick of butter.

Melt the butter. Mix it with the Graham cracker and also sugar. Add a few spoons full of the mix at the end of your cup. It should go to least 1 inch thick. Yet prior to doing so, spray the whole mug with a non stick finish, or brush some thawed butter.

S'More Cake:.
Once more, there is no shame in purchasing ready mix, i.e. fudge brownie mix. This will certainly lessen the preparation time and mess you make. Mix the brownie with the suitable amount of water, milk, eggs, as advised in the box. Now add several spoons full of the fudge mixture. This ought to be about 2 to 3 inches thick. At this point you must be 2/3 into your mason container. Comply with baking directions. This generally means you preheat the oven for 350 levels and after that bake for 20 to 30 mins.

Pillowy Topping:.
Ideal utilize the white marshmallows that are for roasting. Stuff 3 to 4 items onto the mason jar. This ought to take up the rest of the area.
You can roast the Mallows now through your microwave or oven, or you can leave directions for the kids. Again, make certain youngsters recognize that NO METAL PARTS need to be put inside a microwave.

Roast for 1 to 2 mins under tool warm. Finest be on standby at this moment. In this manner you can obtain the mason jar before the marshmallow smudges. An excellent golden brown top coat will do!

Lemon Meringue

- Graham crackers Sugar.
- Butter.
- Lemon custard eggs.
- CASTOR Sugar.
- Fresh lemon (optional).

You will also need graham biscuit crust, so adhere to the guidelines stated above (S'more crust). Next you will need your lemon custard center. Once more, buy any kind of mix and also cook selection. Ideal get 1 item of lemon. You can utilize this to change the level of sour and also sweet by including as much lemon juice and also passion as you want.

Mix the graham crust as advised above. Top with the custard dental filling. You should be 1/2 to 2/3's into your container at this point. Preheat the stove to 350 degrees as well as cook as advised, normally 10 to 20 minutes. It is best to wait on the custard to cook initially, switch off the stove and also let it rest there up until cooled. This prevents the mason container from breaking. As well as enables the oven to cool down just enough so the meringue can bake correctly after.

Meringue Top:.
You will certainly require egg whites and lots of castor sugar. The proportion is 4 egg whites to 1/4 mug CASTOR sugar. Mix with each other as well as defeat continually up until kind peaks.

Pointer: you do not desire any fleck of egg yolk on your egg whites. This will certainly stop it from peaking. If you aren't confident with your yolk separating abilities, make use of a separate dish.

You whisk the egg white up until it's sudsy and white. This will certainly take around 5 to 10 mins. When the resulting whip doesn't drop out of the bowl when you reverse it, you understand it's all set.

Include the castor sugar and blend for a minute; include the staying fifty percent, but this time fold it in for concerning a minute. Folding is a baking skill, similar to a carpenter mixes cement. Take a large spatula, reduced thru the outside border of the bowl and also make a folding motion. Transform the dish and after that do the very same activity over and over once again, for concerning a minute. Foldable allows the combination to be at its fluffiest.

Location the oven on the lowest temperature feasible. Change the meringue topped mason jar. And allow it cook for about 10 to 20 minutes. You don't wish to brown the meringue. At most it needs to be flesh tinted, ideally white. Suggestion: carefully flick your center finger on the custard. You desire a wonderful hollow noise, implying it's solidified thru and also thru.

Apple Tarts

Apple (Any range you like) Sugar.
Cinnamon Nutmeg Butter.
Cornstarch.
Pie crust (readymade) Lemon juice (optional).

This dish is best done on fat however reduced mason jars a.k.a. vast mouth
mason jars 4 to 8 ounces. This is due to the fact that; apple pie is finest
appreciated on a particular ratio of reduced crust, apple tartar, and upper
crust. Pie crust is not so simple to make, that is, if you want it to be
done appropriately. That is why; it is an excellent concept to purchase the
readymade variety. This recipe is for 6 to 8 mugs of mason container apple
tarts.

Suggestion: if this is your first time baking with pie crusts or baking pies for
that matter, attempt various thickness for the crust. It is also a great idea to
bake a few crusts on its very own, simply to see just how it turns out. Your
objective is to have a flaky, split crust.

Reduced Crust:.

Thaw your readymade pie crust, around 10 to 14 ounces will do. You want it to be still cool however flexible. In this manner the flakiness is not jeopardized. Location the crust under portion of your mason container. You desire the crust to cover both all-time low and the sides, with a couple of centimeters excess. This will certainly be used to fold over the leading crust to form a seal.

Apple Filling: There are no shortcuts when making the filling. You want fresh apples of the selection you prefer. The writer chooses Granny Smith. Peel then dice the apple. 3 cups well worth of apples will certainly yield you around 6 to 8 pies, depending upon the dimension of your mason jar. You desire your apple cubes to be a little smaller than the dimension of a normal betting dice.

Mix in 2 tablespoons of brownish sugar, 2 tbsp of cornstarch, 1 tablespoon of cinnamon, as well as a teaspoon of nutmeg. You can likewise include a couple of drops of lemon juice if you desire. Let sit for 5 minutes, then fill your mason jars.

Leading Crust: It's up to you if you want the leading crust to be 1 round or several long, crisscrossing strips. Fold over, then pinch the sides on the excess bottom crust onto the top layer. Cover the top with foil.

Tip: Make certain there are small holes ahead for vapor to run away. If you are utilizing a criss went across pattern, after that deliberately leave tiny voids. If you are using 1 top piece, jab it with a fork two times or 3 times. Cooking.

Pre-heat the stove at 350 levels F. Line up your jars in your baking sheet.
After 25 minutes of cooking, remove the foil, then allow cook for one
more 20 to 30 minutes. This will certainly permit you to brown your leading
crust without shedding the same. Suggestion: this dish puts on different fruit
based pies i.e. pear, pineapple, blueberry, and so on.

For the Health Conscious

Not every mason container recipe need to be undesirable and also pleasant.
You can likewise cook up your own healthy treat, and it doesn't have to be all
that made complex.
Below's exactly how!

Yogurt Goodness

1 litre UHT milk.
unflavored yogurt with live culture Sugar.
Fruits (optional) Powdered milk (optional).
Kitchen thermometer (dip in kind) Ice box.

You want UHT treated so you can forego the challenging heating/pasteurizing
process. Tidy a stainless-steel bowl and also a spatula. Include the milk and
place on low heat. Maintain a slow regular mix. Wait up until the.

temperature hits 120°F (49°C).
Add some sugar to preference. Make certain to utilize a different sampling
spoon each time so you do not taint the milk. Your goal is to make it just a
little bit also pleasant for your taste. Why a little bit also wonderful? This is
since after the culturing procedure most of that sweetness will be gone and
also changed with that sour and appetizing yogurt preference.

Including sugar makes the yogurt thicker. If you desire added thick yogurt,
then add a couple of spoon complete of powdered milk. Now, stir and add the
yogurt up until there are no more noticeable lumps.

Transfer the combination onto your mason jars. At this moment you can add vibrant fruits onto the mix as well as on top for discussion i.e. blueberries, raspberries, strawberries, sliced kiwi, etc. Nicely align inside your colder. Now heat up some water to 120°F (49°C). Place it inside your cooler. Put the water inside the colder. You desire a couple of inches of cozy water. This need to maintain the temperature stable. Close the lid and wait 7 to 10 hours.

Tip: the longer you maintain your yogurt, the tangier it obtains. However as high as possible, don't keep it longer than 12 hours. After you've experienced one container and also are satisfied, enhance as you choose and maintain cooled. This must last for 1 week at most.

Salsa

- Fresh Tomatoes Jalapeno peppers.
- Fresh white onions Salt as well as pepper Lemon juice Garlic.
- Sliced natural herbs like basil or Cilantro.

he salsa you buy from the food store is costly, as well as packed with preservatives. Salsa you make in your home is cheap, extremely easy to make, and also is a wonderful gift suggestion for nacho enthusiasts all over the world.

You can play with the proportion depending on your individual taste. The author likes to have 4 is to 2 is to 1 is to 1: tomatoes, onions, pepper and garlic clove. You can likewise add or not add freshly chopped natural herbs, relying on your individual taste.

You can do it manually, suggesting slice up all the active ingredients with board and knife, or you can make use of a food processor to cut and mix everything. As soon as you've chopped as well as incorporated all the significant components, you then add a tsp of lemon, per ounce of right stuff. Add salt and pepper to taste. Prevent utilizing your hands since you want the salsa to keep longer. To keep longer, can your salsa!

Salad on the Go

True, salad inside a mason jar a little unconventional in terms of a gift. but if you add a twist, it could very well be the best gift idea you can give this holiday season, at least for the health conscious.

And remember, your actual gift is the mason jar and easy salad recipes that go with it. The gift idea is simple; you provide a non decorated mason jar. You fill it with the recipient's salad of choice. Now you create small "post it" like 2 inch by 2 inch strips of paper. Write down different easy and healthy salad recipes. Laminate each card and then string it together.
You then attach the same on another string to the neck of the mason jar.

Add a simple dedication, like: My gift to you is good health. Here's hoping you use these salad ideas for lunch....or words of similar import. Tip: it's best if you add a knitted jacket that covers the mason jar from top to bottom, to facilitate in carrying the same.

For the Adults

You want something that is unique and quirky. If it so happens to contain coffee, alcohol, tobacco, weed (in some states), then all the better. Just make sure that it's legal from the place you are coming form and the place you are sending it to.

Easy Cannabis Cookies

- Readymade cookie batter (any variety)
- Butter
- Dried marijuana leaves
- Choco chips or sprinkles (optional)

It's almost the same as baking cookies, say chocolate chip cookies, but with some weed butter mixed into equation. If you want to prepare the cookie batter from scratch, that's not a problem. But, if you don't have the time or the inclination to do so, then just buy regular cookie dough, some chocolate chips, butter, and some good quality Cannabis.

Why Cannabis butter? Simple, adding fresh or dried weed into your batter won't give you as much kick. Also, the leaves will stick to your teeth! By infusing weed into butter, you get more kick with less teeth and gum picking hassle.

Making the Cannabis Butter is simple; you slowly melt butter using the lowest heat possible. Never let the butter burn and bubble over. When the butter is already in liquid form, you add the weed. If you are not confident about the flame control on your stove, better use the double boiler method. This is simply placing a larger bowl on top of a pot with boiling water.

You can start with a ratio of 10 to 20 grams of weed per 2 sticks of butter (8 ounces). You let the mixture simmer for 10 to 15 minutes.
Turn off the heat and let sit for 30 minutes. You then strain the mixture with a cheese cloth or a regular strainer. Be sure to mass that weed in order to get the last drop of butter.

After this you can throw the weed. There is no more THC in it. THC, being the compound that gives marijuana it's relaxing kick. Now knead the weed butter into your cookie dough. Shape into small bite sized cookies, and top with chocolate chips. Follow the instructions on how hot the oven is and how long it should take to toast.

BTW, you can also gift your friends with Cannabis butter as is! All you need are smaller type mason jars, much like the size of baby food containers 2 to 3 ounces. Add a note attached with a piece of string, on where to use it i.e. hash french bread, hash, omelet, hash pancakes, etc. Tip: don't label it cannabis, hash or marijuana. Label it more discreetly, but whisper to the recipient what it exactly is.

Moonshine Shots

- Moonshine
- Various fruits

If you distill your own moonshine, then you can gift the same to your friends this holiday season. You can also make things more interesting by making moonshine shots. For example, you can soak maraschino cherries into your moonshine.

Let the cherries soak on the moonshine for 1 week at the very least. If cherries is not your thing; how about whole or pitted olives, raisins, berries, or an assortment of such.

Ginseng Liquor

You can also buy Chinese ginseng and add the same into the mix. Buy these from Chinese apothecary shops. Tell the store owner what you intend to do with it, and then ask for ginseng that look, smell, and taste good (relatively speaking) when soaked in alcohol.

- Canned Bacon
- Uncooked bacon
- Wax paper
- Pressurized canning pot (pressure cooker)

Survival prepping is all the rage nowadays. How about you treat your friends with some prepper foodstuff! And when it comes to prepper food, there is nothing more appetizing the canned bacon. It's not going to look good, but it will last for several years.

You will need a wide mouth mason jar, approximately half the size of your bacon strip; some parchment paper and uncooked but cured bacon. What you will do is line up the bacon strips on the parchment paper, one after the other. You then cover the bacon with another parchment paper on top. Fold the parchment, effectively halving the size of each bacon strip. Now roll the bacon strip from one side to the other. It is best to size it so that the fit is snug. Close the lid. Lastly, you actually utilize the mason jar to "can" the bacon (see instructions below).

After canning, if kept inside a shed or your storage room, it should keep for more than a year. If you want it to last longer, then it is best to half cook the bacon in an oven, before you line it up on the parchment paper and roll it. All that is left is for you to label it in a creative way: "Doomsday Bacon: Break in case of emergency". Place the expiration date at 1 year from canning, and you are good to go!

Canning

Canning, using a mason jar refers to the act of using boiling water to take away excess air inside the lid. What this visibly does is create a visible concave on the middle of the lid. As a result food keeps longer, a week or a couple of months even.

You are using mason jars, so you might as well be taught the basics of canning. There is really nothing to it. Canning involves three additional steps. First is the extra strict sanitary procedure i.e. everything that ouches the food needs to be sterilized, and you wipe away excess foodstuff on the on the top portion, of the mason jar. Second, is the extra space you leave, usually a quarter of an inch from the top. Third, you will need a canning pot. This means you completely immerse the filled up mason jars in water, boil it, bottle, lid and all. Wait for the heat to pop down the metal lid. As a general rule, you leave it inside boiling water for 10 to 15 minutes.

What to Can

It is possible to can almost any type of food. Although for longevities sake, it is best to can high acidity type foodstuff, jams, soups, pickled foodstuff, brined meat, etc. After canning you must still keep it stored the same way you would store the food item. For example, canned nuts can be stored on the shelves, but canned soup, must be stored in the freezer. When we say everything, we mean everything. Yes, you can, cam yourself some yogurt, cakes, salads, candies, etc. Although don't expect it to last for more than a couple of weeks.

CAVEAT: When canning raw meat, you need to use a pressure cooker. Boiling foodstuff in water on an ordinary open top pot works well with picking fruits and veggies, BUT NOT MEAT.

Turn on the stove at full burn and wait for steam to come out of the top; now start counting 1o minutes. After that, place the regulator (jiggly thing) on top, wait for it to jiggle, regulate the flame to the minimum amount to keep the regulator jiggling. Now count 70 minutes for pint jars and 90 minutes for quart jars. That is enough time to cook your meat and sterilize everything. Turn of the stove, let it cool for 30 minutes. Remove the regulator. If no steam comes out, wait another 10 minutes, then open the pressure cooker.
Tip: pressure cookers have canning instructions, so follow the same.